∾ FAMILY ∾ ON MISSION

SMALL GROUP
DISCUSSION GUIDE

© 3dm

FAMILY ON MISSION:
Small Group Discussion Guide
© Copyright 2014 by Mike Breen and Ben Sternke

First printing 2014
Printed In the United States of America
1 2 3 4 5 6 7 8 9 10 Printing/Year 16 15 14 13 12 11

Cover Design: Blake Berg
Interior Design: Pete Berg

ISBN: 978-0-9907775-1-9

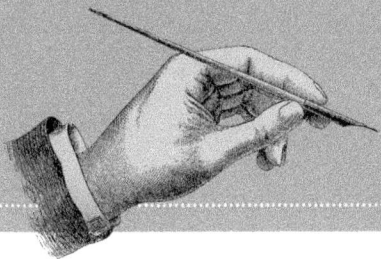

Credits

GENERAL EDITOR:

Ben Sternke

WRITERS:

Art Barrett

Grant Eckhart

Michael Guzman

Seth Richardson

Ben Sternke

∾ Introduction ∾

SO YOU WANT TO BE A FAMILY ON MISSION...

You're in good company. When God set out to save the world, he started with a family and gave them a mission. Around the globe, we all long to be part of a loving family that is changing our world — even if we don't recognize it yet.

This guide will help get you there. We'll give you, the small group leader, the tools and resources you need to facilitate discussion and learning in your small group around the themes discussed in Mike & Sally Breen's book *Family on Mission*.

You'll walk through **10 small group sessions**, each focusing on a particular chapter in *Family on Mission*. Participants read one chapter per week *before coming to the small group meeting*, and the small group session focuses on discussing and digging into the content from the chapter. (It's not necessary for you to have read through the entire book before starting your small group. You can read it chapter-by-chapter along with the rest of your group.)

PREPARING YOUR SMALL GROUP

We recommend you give people at least 2 weeks' notice before you have your first *Family on Mission* small group session. This will give people time to order the book and read the first chapter.

Make sure you:

✍️ Tell them a bit about *why* you want to read through *Family on Mission* together. Cast some vision for why it will be helpful and important for them.

✍️ Tell them **the date** you'll have your first *Family on Mission* small group session.

✍️ Tell them **how to order the book**: Go to http://3dmovements.com, click on STORE, and find *Family on Mission*. You can also order ebooks on all major platforms. (If it works best for your group, you may want want to order books for everyone and hand them out at your next meeting.)

When you are about **one week away from starting**, remind them to read the first chapter before small group next week. You'll probably need to be really clear on this, so people will come prepared to interact about the content they've already read.

ONE TOOL YOU'LL NEED TO BE FAMILIAR WITH: THE TRIANGLE

You don't need to have any special prior knowledge to facilitate a *Family on Mission* small group, but it will be helpful to be familiar with one of our main discipleship tools, the Triangle. (You can find more info on this and 3DM's other discipleship tools in our book *Building a Discipling Culture*.)

The Triangle refers to the **three dimensions of Jesus' life**. As disciples of Jesus, we are seeking to learn how to be like him in character and skill. As we look at his life displayed in the Gospels, we see he lived in "three dimensions," spending time cultivating three important relationships. We see these relationships clearly in Luke 6:12-19:

- **UP toward his Father in heaven** (Luke 6:12). He often spent all night praying, listening and speaking with God.

- **IN toward his disciples** (Luke 6:13-16). He chose twelve to be close to him and to learn from him. Eventually, he called these people his "friends."

- **OUT toward the world** (Luke 6:17-19). He had compassion on the crowds, healed their diseases, and taught them about the kingdom of God.

These three dimensions can be represented through a Triangle:

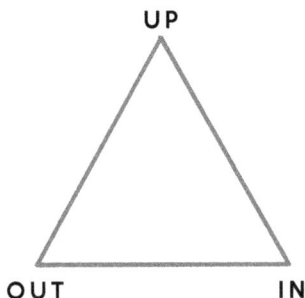

UP

OUT   IN

We follow Jesus UP when we spend time with God in prayer and worship. In this small group guide, **we move UP by facilitating discussion** about the content of the chapter. We also move UP when we pray together as a group.

We follow Jesus IN when we spend time cultivating relationships within the body of Christ. In this guide, **we move IN by participating together in a group activity** that helps us get to know one another and further interact with the content of the chapter.

We follow Jesus OUT when we invest in mission, spending time with the poor or those who don't know Jesus. In this guide, **we move OUT by completing a life application assignment** that helps us integrate the content of the chapter into our lives.

OVERVIEW OF THE SMALL GROUP SESSIONS

Each small group session guide has 9 parts:

1. Arrival / Social Time
2. Assignment Check-in (except for first week)
3. Chapter Synopsis
4. Scriptures to Consider
5. The Main Thought
6. Move UP // Questions for Discussion
7. Move IN // Group Activity
8. Move OUT // Life Application Assignment
9. Closing Prayer

On the following pages, you'll see a suggested timeframe and a brief explanation of how to use each part.

ARRIVAL / SOCIAL TIME *(15 minutes)*

Spend the first 15 minutes or so of your time together catching up and socializing with one another. This is an important part of a small group experience.

ASSIGNMENT CHECK-IN *(5 minutes)*

Each week there will be a simple take home assignment. Spend a few minutes asking about this. Find out if something about the assignment stood out to anyone. You'll need to work hard to keep this part short, as it could easily go long if you have someone who likes to talk! You may only have time for one or two people to share. This is okay.

CHAPTER SYNOPSIS *(2-5 minutes)*

This is a short summary of the content from the chapter that someone reads. This is not a replacement for reading the actual chapter! It simply helps people remember what they've already read earlier in the week (or perhaps in the car on the way to group).

SCRIPTURES TO CONSIDER *(3-5 minutes)*

We have included a few Scripture passages for you, the small group leader, to read ahead of time. You may want to read one or more of these Scriptures in the small group meeting, but don't feel like you need to read them all. They are there for your reference if anyone brings up a related question in the discussion time.

THE MAIN THOUGHT

(Keep this in mind as you facilitate discussion.)
This is simply a one-sentence statement that drives home the big point from the chapter. You won't necessarily read this, but it's what you want people to "get" after this small group session.

MOVE UP // QUESTIONS FOR DISCUSSION

(20-25 minutes)
We'll give you 2-4 questions to ask the group to facilitate discussion. The questions are designed to help people personalize and reflect on the content from the chapter. You want to move past thinking about it "objectively" toward discussing how it could play out in their own lives.

MOVE IN // GROUP ACTIVITY
(20-25 minutes)
Each week you'll have a group activity that (1) helps participants get to know one another better and (2) helps them apply and integrate the content from the chapter.

MOVE OUT // LIFE APPLICATION ASSIGNMENT
(5 minutes)
Explain each week's simple assignment to help them begin to put the content of the chapter into practice.

CLOSING PRAYER *(5 minutes)*
Take a few minutes to gather any prayer requests. (Again, you may have to work hard to keep this short — especially if you have some talkers.) Pray for them, thank God for the time you've had together, and close by praying for the Life Application Assignment.

At the close of each session, always make sure to remind everyone to read the next chapter before your next meeting, and then email them their Life Application Assignment.

GO FOR IT!
That's it! Pretty simple, really. We pray that *Family on Mission* provokes you to follow Jesus as a disciple and join in his mission. We'd love to hear your stories of how it went, as well! Please, email us at info@3dmcentral.com and share your story.

Chapter 1:
⁓ Our Journey to ⁓
Family on Mission

ARRIVAL / SOCIAL TIME
(15-20 minutes)
Spend the first 15 minutes or so of your time together catching up and socializing with one another. This is an important part of a small group experience.

CHAPTER SYNOPSIS *(2-5 minutes)*

Mike and Sally's journey toward the reality we call "family on mission" began with encountering "family OR mission," where they felt forced to choose between one or the other. From there, like many other Christian leaders, they moved on to trying to do both family AND mission, managing margins and creating clear boundaries between "family life" and "mission life." Eventually, they began to learn a new kind of reality called "family ON mission," where they could live one integrated life instead of trying to manage family and mission in separate containers.

SCRIPTURES TO CONSIDER *(3-5 minutes)*

Read any or all of these out loud.

- Genesis 12:1-5
- Ruth 1:1-22

THE MAIN THOUGHT

(Keep this in mind as you facilitate discussion.)
Family OR Mission crushes us. Family AND Mission
exhausts us. But Family ON Mission empowers us to
live out God's calling in the context of community.

MOVE UP // QUESTIONS FOR DISCUSSION *(20-25 minutes)*

What words come to mind when you hear the word
"family"?

_____

_____

_____

_____

What words would you use to describe your family right
now?

_____

_____

_____

_____

Of the three realities described in this chapter, which comes
closest to describing your family?

_____

_____

_____

_____

✎➤ Right now, how optimistic are you about moving into a family on mission reality?

_____

_____

_____

_____

MOVE IN // GROUP ACTIVITY *(20-25 minutes)*

In 3 minutes or less, have each participant tell their family story! *This will feel challenging, but have someone keep time so everyone gets a chance to share. It will be a very quick overview, of course, but this activity will help the group get to know one another more deeply. Even if your group has been meeting for years, you will probably learn something new from each story.*

_____

_____

_____

_____

MOVE OUT // LIFE APPLICATION ASSIGNMENT *(5 minutes)*

Spend 15 minutes this week dreaming about what it would look like to live as a family on mission. What would it look like, feel like, taste like? What would need to change? What would you need to start doing? What would you need to stop doing? What would feel exciting? What would feel challenging?

(Make sure to email everyone the assignment so they don't forget about it, and remind them that you'll start next week by asking them about the assignment.)

_____

_____

_____

_____

CLOSING PRAYER *(5 minutes)*

Take a few minutes to gather any prayer requests. (Remember that you may have to intervene to keep this time short.) Pray for the requests, thank God for the time you've had together, and close by praying for the Life Application Assignment.

Remind everyone to read Chapter 2 before next week's meeting.

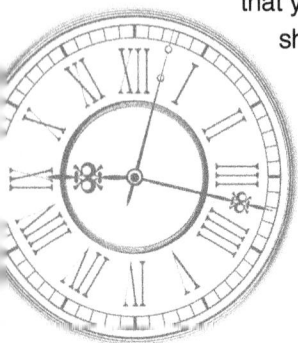

Chapter 2:
∽ Longing for ∾
Family

ARRIVAL / SOCIAL TIME
(15 minutes)

Spend the first 15 minutes or so of your time together catching up and socializing with one another. This is an important part of a small group experience.

ASSIGNMENT CHECK-IN *(5 minutes)*

Ask the group how last week's assignment went. Spend a few moments having people share anything that stood out to them from the assignment. Remember you may have to work proactively to stay within 5 minutes here.

CHAPTER SYNPOSIS *(2-5 minutes)*

Mike describes the cultural earthquake we are currently going through. The time-tested tradition of the extended family has broken down, and we've tried to get by on just the strength of the nuclear family. Interestingly, cultural artifacts such as TV shows are showing us that our longing for extended family has grown significantly over the past couple decades.

SCRIPTURES TO CONSIDER *(3-5 minutes)*

Read any or all of these out loud.

> Genesis 4:1-9
> Genesis 27:1-41
> Psalm 68:4-6

THE MAIN THOUGHT

(Keep this in mind as you facilitate discussion.)
We can see from cultural artifacts all around us that our people all around us deeply desire a sense of belonging in an extended family.

MOVE UP // QUESTIONS FOR DISCUSSION *(20-25 minutes)*

Which of the TV shows mentioned in this chapter is your favorite? Why?

_____

_____

_____

_____

Can you think of any other cultural artifacts (books, TV shows, movies, songs, etc.) that reveal the longing for extended family?

_____

_____

_____

_____

What are some of your favorite "family" moments in movies/ TV shows you've seen recently?

_____

_____

_____

_____

MOVE IN // GROUP ACTIVITY *(20-25 minutes)*

Have everyone in the group take 30 seconds to imagine how family "should be." Then have them quickly write down 3 adjectives that describe how family "should be." Have each participant take 2 minutes to share their 3 words and explain why they chose those words.

_____

_____

_____

_____

MOVE OUT // LIFE APPLICATION ASSIGNMENT *(5 minutes)*

As you go about your week, look at magazines, advertisements, and TV shows, and watch for the "longing for family" we discussed in this chapter. Write down any place you see it, and come ready to discuss one thing you noticed next week.

(Make sure to email everyone the assignment so they don't forget about it, and remind them that you'll start next week by asking them about the assignment.)

_____

_____

_____

_____

CLOSING PRAYER *(5 minutes)*

Take a few minutes to gather any prayer requests. (Remember that you may have to intervene to keep this time short.) Pray for the requests, thank God for the time you've had together, and close by praying for the Life Application Assignment.

Remind everyone to read Chapter 3 before next week's meeting.

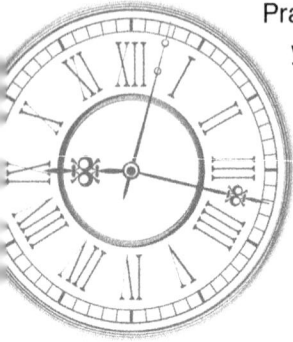

Chapter 3:
⌐ We Were Created ↄ
For This

ARRIVAL / SOCIAL TIME *(15 minutes)*

Spend the first 15 minutes or so of your time together catching up and socializing with one another. This is an important part of a small group experience.

ASSIGNMENT CHECK-IN *(5 minutes)*

Ask the group how last week's assignment went. Spend a few moments having people share anything that stood out to them from the assignment. Remember you may have to work actively to stay within 5 minutes here.

CHAPTER SYNPOSIS *(2-5 minutes)*

Mike challenges the assumption that God's massive project to save the world was given to individuals who are called to carry out that mission by themselves. No! God's Mission is carried out in community through family. The very identity of God is unity in community — Father, Son and Holy Spirit. God himself **is** Family on Mission! God consistently calls a family and gives them a mission, from Adam and Eve, to Noah, to Abraham and Sarah, even to the Apostle Paul and Timothy (among others). Even Jesus refused to do his ministry apart from the context of family on mission.

SCRIPTURES TO CONSIDER *(3-5 minutes)*

Read any or all of these out loud.

- Matthew 3:16-17
- 1 Corinthians 4:14-17
- Genesis 12:1-3

THE MAIN THOUGHT

(Keep this in mind as you facilitate discussion.)
God's methodology for saving the world is a Family on Mission — not an individual going it alone.

MOVE UP // QUESTIONS FOR DISCUSSION *(20-25 minutes)*

- Where in your life are you "going it alone" right now?

_____

_____

_____

_____

- Whether you are single or not, who are the people in your life that you consider to be family?

_____

_____

_____

_____

🍂 What might it be like to picture God as Family (Father, Son, Holy Spirit) when you pray?

_____

_____

_____

_____

🍂 What dream has God placed on your heart for change in the world?

_____

_____

_____

_____

MOVE IN // GROUP ACTIVITY *(20-25 minutes)*

Have everyone in the group take a minute to recall a time in their life when they felt as though they were part of a family (i.e. nuclear family, friends, co-workers, sports teams, neighbors, etc.) accomplishing something together? Then ask them to recall a time when they accomplished something by themselves. Ask everyone to turn to a partner and share the positives and negatives of each of those experiences. Depending on how long it takes for the groups of 2 to share, you may also have certain people share their story with the large group if there is time.

_____

_____

_____

_____

MOVE OUT // LIFE APPLICATION ASSIGNMENT *(5 minutes)*

As you encounter people this week observe whether God might be bringing others around you to be part of your family. Make a list of people who are already part of your family and those that might be part of your family in the future and bring that list with you next week.

(Make sure to email everyone the assignment so they don't forget about it, and remind them that you'll start next week by asking them about the assignment.)

_____

_____

_____

_____

CLOSING PRAYER *(5 minutes)*

Take a few minutes to gather any prayer requests. (Remember that you may have to intervene to keep this time short.) Pray for the requests, thank God for the time you've had together, and close by praying for the Life Application Assignment.

Remind everyone to read Chapter 4 before next week's meeting.

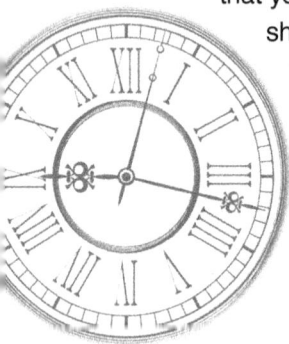

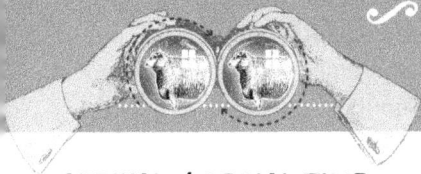

Chapter 4:
❧ Jesus Looks ❧
for Family

ARRIVAL / SOCIAL TIME *(15 minutes)*

Spend the first 15 minutes or so of your time together catching up and socializing with one another. This is an important part of a small group experience.

ASSIGNMENT CHECK-IN *(5 minutes)*

Ask the group how last week's assignment went. Spend a few moments having people share anything that stood out to them from the assignment. Remember you may have to work proactively to stay within 5 minutes here.

CHAPTER SYNPOSIS *(2-5 minutes)*

Jesus' WORDS redefined family around mission. In spite of rejection and silence from his friends and family he didn't abandon the mission God had given him — his WORKS continued. Since Jesus built his family around mission, with those who do God's will, we must follow his WAYS by doing the same.

SCRIPTURES TO CONSIDER *(3-5 minutes)*

Read any or all of these out loud.

❧➤ Mark 3:20-35
❧➤ Luke 4:14-30

THE MAIN THOUGHT

(Keep this in mind as you facilitate discussion.)
If our families aren't focused on the mission of God, we will settle for something easier and less challenging. Our mission must redefine our family.

MOVE UP // QUESTIONS FOR DISCUSSION *20-25 minutes*

What words would describe how Jesus felt after being rejected in Nazareth?

_____

_____

_____

_____

Besides the fear of rejection, what fears do the majority of people face?

_____

_____

_____

_____

What fears affect you the most?

_____

_____

_____

_____

MOVE IN // GROUP ACTIVITY *(20-25 minutes)*

Have everyone in the group share about a time when you have
changed your mission in order to maintain peace in the family -or-
when you have let bitterness from rejection lead you away from
family toward isolation.

_____

_____

_____

_____

MOVE OUT // LIFE APPLICATION
ASSIGNMENT *(5 minutes)*

Jesus didn't schedule meetings to spend
time with his followers; he invited them into
what he was already doing. What are you
already doing that you could invite people
into? What hobbies do you enjoy? What
regularly occurring events are you committed
to? Take fifteen minutes this week to craft a
a two-column list of PEOPLE to invite in, and
THINGS you can invite them into.

*(Make sure to email everyone the assignment so they don't forget
about it, and remind them that you'll start next week by asking
them about the assignment.)*

_____

_____

_____

_____

CLOSING PRAYER *(5 minutes)*

Take a few minutes to gather any prayer requests. (Remember that you may have to intervene to keep this time short.) Pray for the requests, thank God for the time you've had together, and close by praying for the Life Application Assignment.

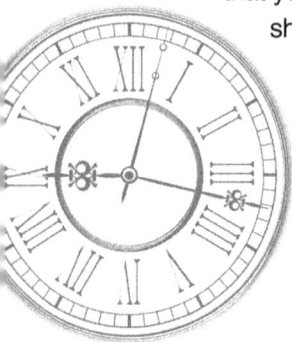

Remind everyone to read Chapter 5 before next week's meeting.

Chapter 5:
ᴔ Jesus Builds ᴔ
a New Family

ARRIVAL / SOCIAL TIME
(15 minutes)

Spend the first 15 minutes or so of your time together catching up and socializing with one another. This is an important part of a small group experience.

ASSIGNMENT CHECK-IN *(5 minutes)*

Ask the group to report about how last week's assignment went. Spend a few moments having people share anything that stood out to them from the assignment. Remember you may have to work proactively to stay within 5 minutes here.

CHAPTER SYNOPSIS *(2-5 minutes)*

Jesus built a family on mission with his friends. As they welcomed Jesus into their own family, Jesus realized his Father was working in them. These friends then became followers — submitting their time and resources to the mission. Eventually, they became family — surrendering their agenda for Jesus' mission to "go and make disciples." This invitation into Jesus' family and family business is still extended to us today.

SCRIPTURES TO CONSIDER *(3-5 minutes)*

Read any or all of these out loud.

ᴔ→ Luke 4:38-5:11
ᴔ→ Matthew 16:13-20
ᴔ→ 1 Peter 2:4-10

THE MAIN THOUGHT

(Keep this in mind as you facilitate discussion.)
Friends *serve* when it's convenient to them. Followers
submit their time and resources for the mission.
Family *surrenders* their agenda to Jesus' mission.

MOVE UP // QUESTIONS FOR DISCUSSION *(20-25 minutes)*

What's the biggest favor you've asked of someone? What's
the biggest favor someone's asked of you?

_____

_____

_____

_____

Does your church have friends? ...followers? ...family?
Which are missing?

_____

_____

_____

_____

How do you and your family most relate to Jesus' family ...
as friends, as followers, or as family?

_____

_____

_____

_____

MOVE IN // GROUP ACTIVITY *(20-25 minutes)*

We often have stories from our past that nostalgically paint the pictures of friends, followers, or family, but we tend to have little evidence of each for the present. Take the time to listen to one another's stories as a way of stirring up a hunger for more. When were some times when someone was a friend, a follower, or a family member to you?

_____

_____

_____

_____

MOVE OUT // LIFE APPLICATION ASSIGNMENT *(5 minutes)*

Friends, followers, and families are identified as we spend time together. If your group has not shared a meal together, set a date to gather for a simple meal. If your group is already eating together regularly, invite other friends who don't know Jesus to your next meal or consider serving together at a local school or nursing home. Brainstorm together this week, and finalize your plan when you meet next week.

(Make sure to email everyone the assignment so they don't forget about it. Email could be a great space to let everyone share their ideas before you make your final plan.)

_____

_____

_____

_____

CLOSING PRAYER *(5 minutes)*

Take a few minutes to gather any prayer requests. (Remember that you may have to intervene to keep this time short.) Pray for the requests, thank God for the time you've had together, and close by praying for the Life Application Assignment.

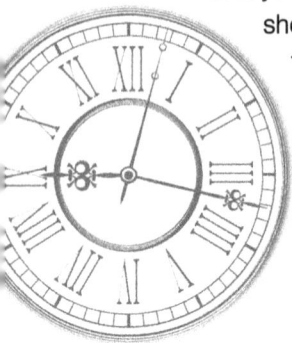

Remind everyone to read Chapter 6 before next week's meeting.

Chapter 6:
Beginning to Build a Family on Mission

ARRIVAL / SOCIAL TIME *(15 minutes)*

Spend the first 15 minutes or so of your time together catching up and socializing with one another. This is an important part of a small group experience.

ASSIGNMENT CHECK-IN *(5 minutes)*

Ask the group how last week's assignment went. Spend a few moments having people share anything that stood out to them from the assignment. Remember you may have to work proactively to stay within 5 minutes here.

CHAPTER SYNOPSIS *(2-5 minutes)*

Mike writes about what it looks like to build a family on mission today. Once we are clear that our family mission should take the shape of Jesus' life, we can begin to discuss the three ingredients in building and multiplying a healthy family on mission. Any family rooted in Jesus will have *spiritual parents* (UP), *predictable patterns* (IN), and *missional purpose* (OUT).

SCRIPTURES TO CONSIDER *(3-5 minutes)*

Read any or all of these out loud.

- Acts 2:42-46
- Hebrews 10:24-25

THE MAIN THOUGHT

(Keep this in mind as you facilitate discussion.)
A healthy family will develop the three elements
found in the family on mission triangle: *spiritual
parents*, *predictable patterns*, and *missional purpose*.

MOVE UP // QUESTIONS FOR DISCUSSION *(20-25 minutes)*

☙ How are the elements pictured in a healthy spiritual family
similar or dissimilar to what we what you see in your own
family?

_____

_____

_____

_____

☙ Why are healthy and effective parents important in a
family? What does family look like when the parents don't
parent well?

_____

_____

_____

_____

☙ What were some of the patterns and purposes in your
family of origin?

_____

_____

_____

Do some families seem to have different purposes? What would you say your family purpose is?

_____

_____

_____

_____

MOVE IN // GROUP ACTIVITY (*20-25 minutes*)

On a scale from 1-10 how would you rate your predicable patterns? Share one encouraging thing you hear God saying to you right now.

_____

_____

_____

_____

MOVE OUT // LIFE APPLICATION ASSIGNMENT (*5 minutes*)

This week rate how you see family on a scale of 1-10 in the three area of parents, patterns and purposes. Come back next week ready to share a couple of your scores and what you hear God saying.

(Make sure to email everyone the assignment so they don't forget about it, and remind them that you'll start next week by asking them about the assignment.)

_____

_____

_____

_____

CLOSING PRAYER *(5 minutes)*

Take a few minutes to gather any prayer requests. (Remember that you may have to intervene to keep this time short.) Pray for the requests, thank God for the time you've had together, and close by praying for the Life Application Assignment.

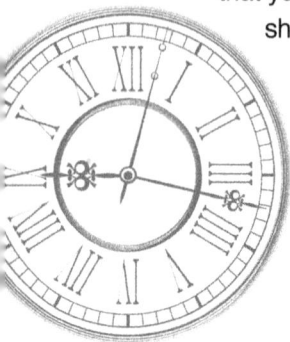

Remind everyone to read Chapter 7 before next week's meeting.

Chapter 7: ✍ Leading as ✍ Spiritual Parents

ARRIVAL / SOCIAL TIME *(15 minutes)*

Spend the first 15 minutes or so of your time together catching up and socializing with one another. This is an important part of a small group experience.

ASSIGNMENT CHECK-IN *(5 minutes)*

Ask the group how last week's assignment went. Spend a few moments having people share anything that stood out to them from the assignment. Remember you may have to work proactively to stay within 5 minutes here.

CHAPTER SYNPOSIS *(2-5 minutes)*

The parent-child relationship is a very close parallel to the rabbi-disciple relationship. Paul consistently describes discipleship through the lens of parenting. Being a spiritual parent like Jesus involves spiritual depth, submission to God, and sacrifice for the good of our family.

SCRIPTURES TO CONSIDER *(3-5 minutes)*

Read any or all of these out loud.

- 1 Corinthians 4: 14-17
- 1 Thessalonians 2:7-8

THE MAIN THOUGHT

(Keep this in mind as you facilitate discussion.)
Jesus invites us to follow his lead through servanthood. Spiritual parents lead their families by cultivating spiritual depth, submitting their agendas to God, and making personal sacrifices for the good of the family.

MOVE UP // QUESTIONS FOR DISCUSSION *(20-25 minutes)*

❧ What are the parallels in today's world for the disciple/rabbi and parent/child metaphors from the New Testament?

_____

_____

_____

_____

❧ What "apprenticeship" or "follow me to learn" experiences have you had personally?

_____

_____

_____

_____

❧ Have you ever had someone join your family like Sally described about Jo (and later Chris) Saxton? What was that like?

_____

_____

_____

MOVE IN // GROUP ACTIVITY *(20-25 minutes)*

☙➤ Think of an example of when someone gave of their own time and talent to help you get better at something. Tell the group about that learning experience.

_____

_____

_____

_____

☙➤ Share with the group a story of someone who has left a lasting impression on you. What was one thing that impressed you most about how they led and invested in your life?

_____

_____

_____

_____

☙➤ Why were these leaders able to do what they did to serve you? What made them different from the other people around you?

_____

_____

_____

_____

MOVE OUT // LIFE APPLICATION ASSIGNMENT *(5 minutes)*

Before you go, let's recall Sally's story about Chris and Jo Saxton. Ask God to show you who is orienting toward your life. Let's come back next week and share one place outside your immediate family you think God may want you to step into spiritual parenthood or to realize you already are a spiritual parent.

(Make sure to email everyone the assignment so they don't forget about it, and remind them that you'll start next week by asking them about the assignment.)

_____

_____

_____

_____

CLOSING PRAYER *(5 minutes)*

Take a few minutes to gather any prayer requests. (Remember that you may have to intervene to keep this time short.) Pray for the requests, thank God for the time you've had together, and close by praying for the Life Application Assignment.

Remind everyone to read Chapter 8 before next week's meeting.

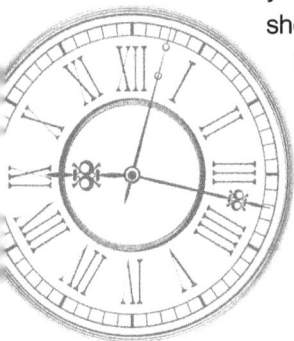

Chapter 8:
∽ Predictable ∾
Patterns

ARRIVAL / SOCIAL TIME *(15 minutes)*

Spend the first 15 minutes or so of your time together catching up and socializing with one another. This is an important part of a small group experience.

ASSIGNMENT CHECK-IN *(5 minutes)*

Ask the group how last week's assignment went. Spend a few moments having people share anything that stood out to them from the assignment. Remember you may have to work proactively to stay within 5 minutes here.

CHAPTER SYNPOSIS *(2-5 minutes)*

Not only do families on mission need *spiritual parents* in order to flourish, they also need *predictable patterns*. When we look at Jesus' life, we see that he led his followers in regular, fixed rhythms of life such as prayer, table fellowship, and public ministry. These patterns also became the patterns of the early church. Predictable patterns serve as fixed points that help orient the family toward what is most important. Mike and Sally describe how predictable patterns characterized by love, discipline, and freedom led to flourishing in their biological and extended *oikos*.

SCRIPTURES TO CONSIDER *(3-5 minutes)*

Read any or all of these out loud.

- Deuteronomy 6:4-9
- Acts 2:42-47

THE MAIN THOUGHT

Keep this in mind as you facilitate discussion.
Predictable patterns are about creating the stability needed for nurturing the covenantal identity that leads to a life of significance.

MOVE UP // QUESTIONS FOR DISCUSSION *(20-25 minutes)*

- Have you experienced predictable patterns more as freedom or bondage? Were they more like dead ritualism or life-giving rhythms?

_____

_____

_____

_____

- Reflect on the patterns that *already* exist in your family. What do those patterns reveal about what is most important to your family?

_____

_____

_____

_____

☙ Do you "parent" more naturally in freedom, like Sally, or discipline, like Mike? What would it look like to calibrate more of the other in your family?

_____

_____

_____

_____

☙ What is the difference between discipline and punishment? How would you know which is being cultivated in your family?

_____

_____

_____

_____

MOVE IN // GROUP ACTIVITY _(20-25 minutes)_

Have everyone write down one example of experiencing love through discipline or freedom in a family context. Then, ask a few members to share and discuss why that example was meaningful to them.

_____

_____

_____

_____

MOVE OUT // LIFE APPLICATION ASSIGNMENT (5 minutes)

Think about one predictable pattern you'd like to start or be *more intentional* about with your family. Share your idea with the group and explain why you picked it. Try out that pattern this week. Come ready next week to discuss both failures and successes. Remember, patterns take time to become part of the fabric of your life!

(Make sure to email everyone the assignment so they don't forget about it, and remind them that you'll start next week by asking them about the assignment.)

_____

_____

_____

_____

CLOSING PRAYER (5 minutes)

Take a few minutes to gather any prayer requests. (Remember that you may have to intervene to keep this time short.) Pray for the requests, thank God for the time you've had together, and close by praying for the Life Application Assignment.

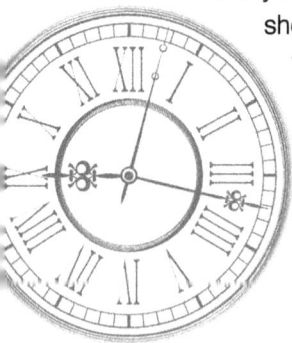

Remind everyone to read Chapter 9 before next week's meeting.

Chapter 9:
∾ Moving Out ∾
in Missional Purpose

ARRIVAL / SOCIAL TIME *(15 minutes)*

Spend the first 15 minutes or so of your time together catching up and socializing with one another. This is an important part of a small group experience.

ASSIGNMENT CHECK-IN *(5 minutes)*

Ask the group how last week's assignment went. Spend a few moments having people share anything that stood out to them from the assignment. Remember you may have to work proactively to stay within 5 minutes here.

CHAPTER SYNOPSIS *(2-5 minutes)*

Chapter Nine reaches into the heart of flourishing as a family on mission. Along with *spiritual parents* and *predictable patterns*, families on mission need a *missional purpose*. In fact, a *missional purpose* is the integrating principle that makes any family on mission work. Mike describes how the grand purpose of any family on mission is to multiply the life of Jesus into others by living into the words, ways, and works of Jesus. Under that grand vision for mission, Mike unfolds why families on mission also need a specific *missional purpose* and how to get started discerning what that is.

SCRIPTURES TO CONSIDER *(3-5 minutes)*

Read any or all of these out loud.

- Matthew 28:16-20
- 1 Peter 2:9-12
- Colossians 3:12-17

THE MAIN THOUGHT

(Keep this in mind as you facilitate discussion.)
A clear *missional purpose* gives families a framework for orienting everything they do — even mundane things — around multiplying the life of Jesus.

MOVE UP // QUESTIONS FOR DISCUSSION *(20-25 minutes)*

- Why is listening for the *words* of Jesus fundamental to living a life on mission?

_____

_____

_____

_____

- How can we tell if our *ways* align with the *ways* of Jesus?

_____

_____

_____

_____

☙ What family decision seems most difficult for you right now? What factors presently motivate how that decision will be made for your family?

_____

_____

_____

_____

MOVE IN // GROUP ACTIVITY _(20-25 minutes)_

Brainstorm different families or organizations (Christian or otherwise) that stick out to you because they operate with clear mission and purpose. Make a list of things that characterize those families or organizations. Have everyone share which characteristics seem most compelling to them and why.

_____

_____

_____

_____

MOVE OUT // LIFE APPLICATION ASSIGNMENT *(5 minutes)*

Plan some intentional time with your family (maybe 10 minutes during each dinner this week, to discuss the passions, possessions, and problems that God has put on your heart for your context. Celebrate these discoveries as God's gift; then, begin to explore where they converge. Toward the end of the week, take a stab at formulating a family missional purpose statement, and come prepared to share it with the group next week.

(Make sure to email everyone the assignment so they don't forget about it, and remind them that you'll start next week by asking them about the assignment.)

_____

_____

_____

_____

CLOSING PRAYER *(5 minutes)*

Take a few minutes to gather any prayer requests. (Remember that you may have to intervene to keep this time short.) Pray for the requests, thank God for the time you've had together, and close by praying for the Life Application Assignment.

Remind everyone to read Chapter 10 before next week's meeting.

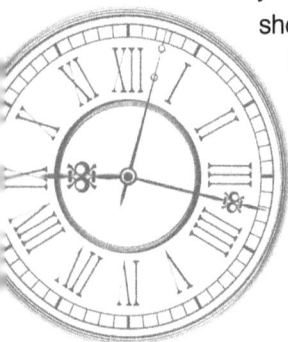

Chapter 10:
∾ Encouragement ∾
for the Journey

ARRIVAL / SOCIAL TIME
(15 minutes)
Spend the first 15 minutes or so of your time together catching up and socializing with one another. This is an important part of a small group experience.

ASSIGNMENT CHECK-IN *(5 minutes)*
Ask the group how last week's assignment went. Spend a few moments having people share anything that stood out to them from the assignment. Remember you may have to work proactively to stay within 5 minutes here.

CHAPTER SYNPOSIS *(2-5 minutes)*
Sally shares their journey of moving "as a pack" to America to start a new adventure of mission. Through the ups and downs of the journey, they simply sought to do normal family stuff with their wider *oikos*. Sally shares at the end that 2 Corinthians 12:9 has become a life verse for them, where Jesus tells the apostle Paul during a difficult time, "My grace is sufficient for you, for my power is made perfect in weakness."

SCRIPTURES TO CONSIDER *(3-5 minutes)*

Read any or all of these out loud.

- 2 Corinthians 12:1-10
- Hebrews 11:1-12:3

THE MAIN THOUGHT

Leading a family on mission is never easy, and often we will be signing up for *more* difficulty and trouble because of it. But we hold onto the promise that God's power will be with us and that the trouble will be worthwhile. It's a great investment.

MOVE UP // QUESTIONS FOR DISCUSSION *(20-25 minutes)*

- Sally talks about moving in response to God's call, but there are other reasons that people move. Why has your family moved in the past?

_____

_____

_____

_____

- Moving to a different country is a huge step of faith, and not one that most people are called to do, of course. But what is one small step of faith you think God might be leading your family to take?

_____

_____

_____

Sally mentions a "life verse" that has been important to her and Mike. Are there any "life verses" that have been important for you and your family? What makes them significant for you?

_____

_____

_____

_____

MOVE IN // GROUP ACTIVITY *(20-25 minutes)*

Have everyone write down one step of faith they want to take toward being a family on mission. Then, one by one, have each person share their faith step, and have the person on their right pray for them. Then the person who just prayed shares their faith step, and the person to *their* right prays for them, and so on…

_____

_____

_____

_____

MOVE OUT // LIFE APPLICATION ASSIGNMENT *(5 minutes)*

Decide what's next for your group! You've all made statements of faith about where you feel God is calling your family on mission. This is your assignment for next time: Do something this week that moves you toward your faith step.

Next we will celebrate all God has done. Come ready to report how you took a step of faith and how it went.

(Make sure to email everyone the assignment so they don't forget about it, and remind them that you'll start next week by asking them about the assignment.)

_____

_____

_____

_____

CLOSING PRAYER *(5 minutes)*

Take a few minutes to gather any prayer requests. (Remember that you may have to intervene to keep this time short.) Pray for the requests, thank God for the time you've had together, and close by praying for the Life Application Assignment.

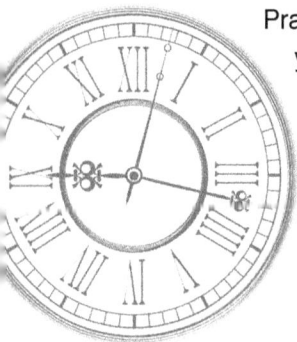

Final
Celebration

CELEBRATION GATHERING

This final gathering in the Family on Mission Small Group experience is a celebration of all God has done during the past few weeks. So throw a party! Have everyone bring food and drinks to share, and have a meal together.

ARRIVAL / SOCIAL TIME *(15 minutes)*

Spend the first 15 minutes or so of your time together catching up and socializing with one another, allowing time for people to arrive and get their food ready.

THANKSGIVING *(10 minutes)*

Have everyone share one thing they are thankful for from the past few weeks in small group.

EAT TOGETHER *(30 minutes)*

Enjoy a meal together!

DEBRIEF *(15 minutes)*

End the meal together by giving people an opportunity to share their step of faith from last week, and how it went.

CLOSING PRAYER *(5 minutes)*

Take a few minutes to gather any prayer requests. Pray for these requests, thank God for the time you've had together, and close by praying for future fruitfulness as you all build your families on mission!

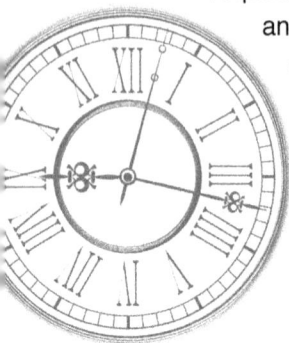

HOW TO GO FURTHER

If you want to explore discipleship and mission further, try these **next steps**:

- Join our email newsletter (3dmovements.com/newsletter). You'll get weekly updates and tips on discipleship, leaders, and mission.

- Check out our book *Oikonomics*.

- Check out our book *Building a Discipling Culture*.

- Find out more about Coaching http://3dmovements.com/coaching. It's a great way to engage in the journey of discipleship yourself and learn to take others on the same journey. It's about learning to make disciples who can make disciples.

- Attend a *Family on Mission* workshop. Check the website for upcoming dates.

- Finally, visit our website (3dmovements. com) to explore more resources for discipleship, leadership, and mission.

3DMovements.com